welcome to
the ice cream social

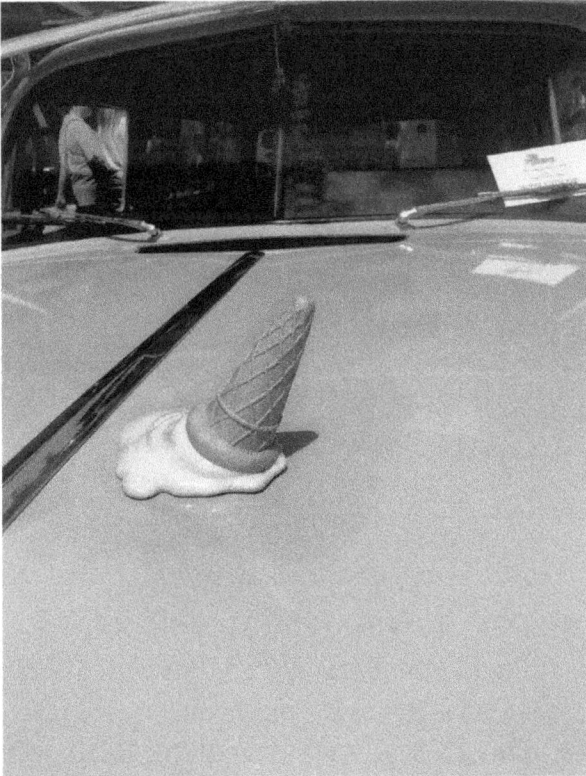

by CA Hurley

for carol

table of contents

welcome to
the ice cream social

ANXIOUS ALGORITHMS

stolen oxygen

you did it
again!

how do
so many organs

even fit
in such a
tiny chest?

this is ridiculous.

just a couple
normal breaths

is all
i am asking for

but with every inhale
i only exhale
more inhale

until
my insides have
repelled **off a cliff**

does

t h i s

make-any-sense?

IN THE OPEN

it was freeing

being a
tiny bird

in the first steps
towards earth;

i am a
tiny bird

with one foot
forward
off a cliff

with no wonder
with only instinct;

i am a
tiny bird

with one foot
forward
toward earth

and nothing else.

SOMETIMES, DIRT LOOKS YUMMY

i salivate

while
you talk

with beer
dripping
off your
bottom lip

talking
fast

looking at
my tits

not noticing
that i have noticed
your eyes

i brush my thigh
slowly

and you keep at it

talking
faster

16

i pull my elbows
in

bending
forward
toward
the table

i am
thirsty, sip.

a bit of
vodka
falls
into my shirt

you,   *"mmm"*
and shut up.

IT IS A 5 DOLLAR CREDIT LIMIT

*"what' s your dollar shots
then?"*

*"i don' t know, something
vodka, and··· you' ll be ok. "*

i always had
perfect teeth

people would
stop me, and
be like, girl

your smile
you' ve had braces?

i' d be like, nope
and i was always
proud of that.

then i started smoking
cigarettes

and now, i
smile
less
and **stress**

more

over
my
health

and constantly think
life is
funny
like that.

and you' re right

whatever
the fuck
that shot
is made of

i' ll be
alright.

A THANK YOU NOTE FROM BED

the books
the papers
the magazines
the websites

they all say
stress kills

the news
the documentaries
the movies
the cartoons

they all say
stress kills

yet, here i am
reading it
hearing it
with knotted shoulders
and a pulsating **brain**

yet, here you are (reading me)
absorbing it
dissolving it
then giving me knotted hair
and a pulsating heart (instead).

MANIPULATING MALNOURISHED MOLECULES

in through the mouth and
out through the nose

who even knows what
my **brain** cells are doing

really, who even cares

as long as
i am happy, right?

in through the mouth and
out through the nose

i think this is about as close
as i will get to what i want

the smoke blows in
all directions
fogging my
cognitive thinking.

in through the mouth and
out through the nose

i am blinking and
sinking into this chair

i want to forget
there was a time
when i wasn' t
glued to this chair.

in through the mouth and
out through the nose

i want
anything else

even if it' s
just rubbing
this piece of
felt.

in through the **mouth** and
out through the nose

why would someone
cover a throw pillow in felt

we all
need to
sort ourselves
out.

THE VODKA GOT ME, AGAIN

it' s five to one and i am
sitting out front

across from the police station at
this bar and there is
a cigarette falling out of
my **mouth** as i type this
into my phone.

i just know
it needs to get out:

i threw up on
a mirror in the bathroom

i did it as i was standing
there, staring at myself

wondering if this
release is worth it

because i know by now, i should
feel euphoric, yet
i just feel tragic

i feel like
maybe i just booty **called** myself.

THE FAIR

i saw
you **called**

left a message
and everything.

wow!

but i
am busy

indefinitely

spinning in
circles

while pushing
the lever

up
and
down

on my
office
chair.

it almost feels like
the fair.

i close my eyes
and let the hand
holding my **doob**
fall to my waist

this feels so much more
than anything

you ever
gave me.

so, i have decided
to give myself

completely to
this moment

this feeling.

CATCHING A RIDE

perfect circles
rise from
a poorly rolled **doob**
held in
a worn-out hand;

though i am
far from perfect

my smoke rings
are

and that is enough
for me to feel
perfect, too

even if
it is only for

the lifespan of
a **smoke** ring.

DOOBIE DIALOGUE

"you would be
the first to go if
this was a horror film"

i choked out
the **smoke** i was
holding in

into the
disgusting, cold air

but i won' t complain
all of us made a pact this summer
to not complain this winter.

i started coughing, since
i really wasn' t
expecting the smoke
to **escape** like that

so
suddenly

and because of the cold
my throat
instantly
iced over

and a sip
of my drink

only made it
worse, of course.

and when i
finally
regained
my breath

i whispered,
*"tell me how
you really feel, dickhead."*

the last bit
being a little louder
than the rest.

HAVING TO REROLL IT

rogue stems poke
holes in a
tightly rolled joint
compromising the
mission in my hand

... allowing words
like smoke
to **escape** me
to escape ink

... allowing only tiny
portions of what was
meant for my lungs
to even make it
meant for my redemption
meant to be sacrificial
for all the trees i have
demolished talking to you

... allowing it all to be lost
the person i am
the head full of
somersaulting sonnets
the promised medicinal properties
the possibility of
something better

than
starting
over.

AN ITALIAN BABY SHOWER

i feel sick
and i know it's
my own fault:
starting with a beer
that lead to another
and another, all before
i left my house
now i am here
and i feel
sick, babies are
cute—i don't think
that's why···
your signature drink
is what got me—i think
it's a boy!
now have some gin
and blueberry
then
stand around a **pool**
and wait for
the first person
to fall in
have a beer, it's
on tap!
out front
a blunt
a few ciggys

no biggy, if
my stomach
wasn't being
such
a cunt, i need
to pee
but
we are leaving
i take a bump, then
slide into
your backseat
i think i
was supposed to
be taking it easy
but my blueberry drink
has me
feeling sleazy
i think i'll
keep going

it ain't my kid

after all
i ain't the one pregnant.

THE POOL MAN & I

a blue shirted
ass

waving his
stick around

pretending to
be king:

it is saturday
hot and sticky

it is my day off
from doing nothing

so, take off your
weird cotton mask

hat, too
and relax

what spf
do you use?

did your father clean pools
too?
do you even like to swim?

c' mon
sit down
and pretend to
be my friend

c' mon
the **pool** is
clean enough
you are done

c' mon
sit down
and **stop**
blocking the sun.

INSTEAD

you are in my head
and though i like you, a lot
stop! get in my **bed.**

YOU SAY QUIRK WHILE I FIGHT ADDICTION

i cannot
tell you why

only that it is something i do
a lot.

knocking on my bedroom door
at 3 in the morning
sleepy eyes and messy hair
my ma would demand
in what i remember
to be the angriest
yet calmest voice possible
the only person i have ever
witnessed to do this
  "what in the world, christie!
  it's the middle of the night.
  go. to. sleep. now!"

i would plead that i
couldn't sleep
that things weren't right
that nothing felt right

still, she would force
me to **bed**

no matter what odd position
the bed currently resided

no matter how many
books, dolls, and clothes were
on top

still, she expected me
to get in.

and i always would
my ma was the law.

but when she would turn
the lights off
and i heard her
bedroom door close

i would jump out of bed
and tiptoe back to action

only quieter this time

until everything
was rearranged
and somehow
better.

REMEDY REMINDERS

there is a painting
that sits on my desk

behind the typewriter
i am using now.

i made it back in 2003
sitting in an art class
in the building **my ma**
once sat in.

way back when
this all

everything that rotates
in my head

way back when
i controlled that.

it' s in the style of those old
florida highwaymen, on an
upson board
and it was horrible

i mean, it is horrible.

despite
the globs of acrylic
i had failed to blend in

the waves that looked like
angry white earthworms

the palm leaves resembling
monster hands

the trees being
toothpicks

despite all that

i kept it.

i have
kept it

through college
through the years after
through countless apartments
through all the different men.

i have
kept it

reminding myself to be shit at some
things, don't go forcing anything.

THE ARCHITECT

you let me build a
dream home with little **toothpicks**

near **hungry** quicksand.

A PLACE WHERE THE GRASS IS GREENER

i saw your best friend
in the grocery store

i was **hungry.**

he looked well
telling me about
his new job
and the classes
he is taking at **school**

he was hungry.

neither of us bothered
to mention you.

NO JOKE

i knew this
girl when i was
away at
university, a
nice girl but
not so smart:

we went to
the lake district
and she asked if
it was the sea

we went to
a pub and she
would get
drunk off rose'
and ask if
the states
were like
in the movies
do we all live
in mansions
and drive
fancy cars?
i let her down
with no, something
i don' t think

she hears often

when we would
get high on my
couch she would
tell me that
school wasn' t
really
for her, neither
was
a job, but
she knew
girls in the port
getting paid
to
have kids

she
wanted
that.

⋯ a few years later
her name
came up
and i asked

they told me
she was
living down by
the docks

with twins
getting **money**
from
the dole.

i sighed
out a
congrats

on her
big win.

sometimes
dreams do
come true

in case
you were
wondering.

RICH IN WHAT?

money
over
sanity

i continue to
choose

money
over
sanity

i would ask
for someone' s hand
in sorting out
the crazy
in my head

but that
ain' t
in
my vocabulary

i will instead
statically
watch
everyone
else

come and go
with ease.

who knows
what
that means

for me, left here

with something
so easily
burnt down.

please!

take away
all my
lighters

the unknown is
becoming
a bit scary.

YOU'RE A BITCH

yes, i burn.

i know you think it
otherwise, thinking
i am made of ice

well, here is
some advice

perhaps **everyone**
you have ever met
is not exactly who
you thought

perhaps everyone
is a pretender

a liar
too.

CATS

perhaps it is because
i am high
nah
i am always high.

it is probably because
i am drunk
wait no
i have only had
3 or 4 beers.

there are
none left.

6
i had 6 beers.

yeah···
it is because
i am **drunk** that

i have been sitting here for
the past twenty minutes
watching a cat
toss a rubber band
about the mess she made
by knocking over the trash.

PARALLELING TO THE WORD FUCK

out
of
control

which isn' t ideal
fuck, it' s real

you
are
back.

a knock
on my door

it' s 4
in the fucking
afternoon

i am not
drunk enough
for this

and anyone
who usually reads
my stuff knows
this isn' t natural

i am a
little off
and it is
you...

the only guy to
ever
cum
inside me

that is
disgusting, sorry.

life
sometimes
ain' t like
the movies.

SHOWER BEER

clear? things haven' t
been like that for
a while now

it' s all a
little hoppy as
i scotch my way
between

scalding hot water
and a
12 ounce can with
the cold sweats

just hoping to
find a sip that will
make me forget you

just **trying** to
get through a shampoo
without you.

I'M CHOKING

i'm **trying** to
do this fast

puff
puff

please
do not
make
me
pass

this has been
rolled so poorly and
if i let any bit go

i
know
i
will
be
left
with   o
only
                    m   k
s

                                                    e.

MY 420 POEM

bong rips?

bing.
bong.

it is a doob,
dude.

pass that
and
do not
bogart it

for we are all
waiting to
hit it.

GIRLS AND THEIR MIRRORS

i spend
too much time
getting ready:

too much time
preparing the workspace

cleaning and
organizing the desk

rearranging the pictures
on the wall

looking through
old notebooks

rolling
doobies

then smoking them
while **waiting**

rolling another
and another, before i will
pick up a finger and
stroke a single key.

i spend too much time
avoiding you:

too much time
distracting my thoughts with
mundane motions for my hands

thinking about other boys
the ones that give me **attention**
i'll pretend to like it

so, i look at my phone
start scrolling through
your pictures, then the girl's
pictures that last commented on
yours, and then her sister's

so, i call my brother
ask if he wants to go
to the bar, and also if
he could pick me up
my brakes are shot—i need a
new car

and when we get there,
i'll see you, and i'll act
like i barely know you
and you don't like that

you'll say, you've been calling

why haven' t i called back
i' ll respond with, i never got a
call (but i did)

you' ll say, i should really start
listening to my voice mails
you' ve been alone every night this
week, thinking about me.

too much time
on my pride:

too much time
on these words
these books

all these mantras i
repeat when i' m drifting to sleep

why can' t i just give in
why am i such a jerk
why won' t i let myself be happy
why does love feel like nothing
why do you say you love me
why don' t i flinch
why does jealousy and hate
give me the goosebumps?

i' m so dumb, spending all
this time on: nothing.

YOU TALK IN YOUR SLEEP

my eyelids were fluttering
until i heard a chatter

you babbling on
a crooked little brook

my **attention** snapped straight up
an exclamation point;

i am addicted to your secrets
the ones you spill in the night

and perhaps what i do
isn' t right

but right now
it' s the only time

i can get you
to **talk**

which is
fair enough to me.

ONE OF MANY SCARS

you like
>to **talk** about
>my hair

you like
>it brown

you like
>to talk about
>my mouth

you like
>that i "talk back"

you like
>to point out
>my mistakes

you like
>to fondle the thoughts
>i have of us

you like
>to play

you like
>that i like
>to play, too

you like
>to say
>you don' t know me

you like
>when i send you
>dirty pictures

you like
        when i don't
        text you for days
you like
        when i text at
        4am saying, *"hey"*
you like
        everything
        i do
you like
        everything
        you do
you like
        when i compliment you
you like
        when i say, it is only you

you
you
you
you

you
are a
distant **memory**, and

we both like it
best, this way.

RACCOONS

whole neighborhoods, together
silently pretend they are
somewhere or someone else

and so do you
but i can' t

not with my mind rabidly
tearing through any **memory** of
us left **outside**

hoping i find
a meal there

hoping i find
anything there.

STOCKHOLM SYNDROME

feather on
the porch floor

white and black with a
subtle trace of light brown

a cat lives inside the walls
i have set for her

she has
never tasted a bird.

found it **outside**
my front door

weathered and a bit worn
i brought it to the sink for

a quick wash but turned
the faucet off.

soap is for me
not her.

i threw the likely
disease ridden body part

towards her
waiting feet.

a few minutes is all it took
and it was destroyed

reduced to
a battered toy

she rubbed her head against
my legs, to say, thanks.

i rested my vision on
the palm trees outside and

thought about
all the things

i
have yet

to
taste.

FLORIDA

during the hot and humid
days of december

sitting under ceiling fans
and air conditioner vents

i would watch the news about
snow in the north and out west

the kids running around
making things with ice

catching flakes on their
tongues, it made me jealous.

i didn' t know what it was like
and i still don' t

but this reminds
me of that

i think it might
feel really close:

lifting my hand to
my mouth

lips and a doob
light the meteorological match

and
i watch

swirls of smoke take
control of the atmosphere

sprawling shapes fall
towards my head

wanting to
capture it all

i stick out my tongue
and **taste** it, too.

it's like christmas here
in my living room (**fuck**)

that's some good
weed right there.

FUNNEL CAKE DRUNK

8-year-old me
would have figured that
18-year-old
me would have told the
28-year-old
version of myself to
fuck off, by now

but
it
hasn' t.

therefore, fuck you

if you
don' t like cats.

that is just
not ok

love 'em all
you twat, i have managed that.

the roach
i killed at work.
the fish
i won at the fair.

and definitely those two
damn cats
that have
found a
home in what
i call, home.

yah, sure
i wanted dogs

but at least
these don' t talk back.

fuck, that' s
a **lie,** they do.

oh, just fuck off, if you don' t like
cats.

PLAYING WITH THE WEST

it's a
lie, everything.

my ma always said, if it
ain' t the truth, it' s a
lie.

and i
am spinning.

laid out
on your floor, after
just one night
with ya, looking at

brand-new concrete ceilings, i
think i might
just know what

i think i mean.

i mean, i think you, you do
things to me.

the stars
seem
a little

brighter here in
the desert, reminds me
of spain, and man

i am
trying so hard
to blame
these sparks
on the wine.

but i know
it' s you.

and you
have known
longer
than i.

BOOGIE MAN

thumb pinky
thumb ring
thumb middle
thumb pointer

thumb pointer
thumb middle
thumb ring
thumb pinky

ten times until
you are no **longer**
there

close my **eyes** and
repeat it

ten times until
i no longer
care.

KEEPING IT COOL

i should have been
watching your lips but i
couldn' t take my **eyes**
off our ceiling fan and
though it was on
the highest setting because
that' s how we like it

i was seeing it in
slow-motion

and your **voice**
was muffled in with the
whooping of unmaintained
blades

laid out
played out

i wondered if i
liked the fan blasting
or if
i only liked it, knowing
you liked it.

FATALITY

plans
and expectations

slapped down by a
particle of dust.

a quick blow
a cotton swab

prayers to the
nintendo gods

mixed with a few
politically incorrect
tricks to get
the game in

frustration
at eight

but when
the **voice**
barreled
through the
television **saying**
"finish him"

the struggle, the
patience
became
worth it.

forward
down
forward
high punch

i
think
i
win.

BUZZ KILL

flat on
my back

there is
a rip in
i think it is
a paper chinese lantern

i don' t know
though.

my fingers run
through
a forest of
cuddles
beneath me

your voice comes in **saying**
"you look strange
how are you feeling?"

i whisper, *"fine"*

you laugh and ask
 "has it kicked in yet?"

then put
your hand on
my **head**
and pet me

like
a dog

i moved over

i think
i moved over
  "don' t pet me, " i slurred.

you started
laughing, louder this time
and told the other guy

i think
his name was
jason

you told
jason
they had, in fact
kicked in.

then started talking about
the last time you ate one of
jason' s edibles.

YOU ONLY

crawl inside my **head**:
make a bed, **stay,** have some tea
with the voices there.

THEY OTHER SIDE

you peak your
head in. i catch it
from the corner of my eye

doob in mouth, lighter in hand
i pause, *"what's up?"*

a little drunk, you say nothing—just
stare, just **stay** there
flapping your long eyelashes
an envy of mine
you fall a bit into the wall
and a bit into the door

i ask again, *"what's up?"*

you step into the room
exposing a rolling rock can
"is this what you
plan on doing
with your night?"

i flip the typewriter on, and say
"yeah"

making you pout, and whine, *"i am bored"*

76

i light the doob
and start flipping
through my notes

"i am bored," you say again.

i close the notebook
look at you
"why don' t you play some music

i really need
to write

we partied last night
when i was supposed to
be writing, remember?"

"oh, alright," you say
then ask, *"can i at least*
type the first sentence?"

frustrated, i bark out, *"no!"*

then naturally
feel bad
and follow with
"oh, fine"

you smile and come closer
sitting in the chair with me

*"you can pick the **title**,"* i snap

thinking it over
for a minute
you then ask
"this is like a computer, right?"

i nod and take a drag of
the doob, looking away.

when you finish
you get up and walk off

i look down
confused, and yell out
*"what does
'they other side'
mean?"*

a *"fuck!"*
came rushing back in from
the living room

but you didn' t bother
to follow it.

and that is
why i like you.

COMING TO GRIPS

i am ripping my
hair out when i
think of you
ripping my
hair out;

sometimes i write the
title first
then make up the rest;

sometimes i **forget** that
substance is
what matters most.

oops···

NO MILK NO SUGAR NO PROBLEMS

my first cup of
coffee

was all
milk and sugar

sweet
but still bitter

i didn' t touch it again
until i was older.

as the
years went

and my mind
and my sleep

so
did the milk

so
did the sugar

sometimes now
i **forget** the store

and drink it
black.

i feel this way
about you, too

friends
lovers
enemies
lovers
broken
lovers
broken
broken
lovers

we are inconsistent
but in the end

you
were all i needed.

just you
just the coffee.

LAZY WAYS

without the thrown rock
you hopscotched your way
to the roadside shade
 "holy fuck"

you rubbed your foot
and watched me do the same
 *"that' s fucking
white hot, "* you added.

i looked down at
the **black** asphalt
then back at you
 "that doesn' t make sense. "

you rolled your eyes and
turned towards our street
walking in the grass
 *"it' s an expression
you ass. "*

i followed a few steps behind
trying to light my last **ciggy**
with a waterlogged bic
 *"just say what you mean
next time. "*

LIGHTING BOTH ENDS

i hate how weak i am.

one little **ciggy** burn and
i have to make sure my
hand stays away from soap.

i am a wimp.

and we both know it.

i am laying low in
the front seat of your **car**
shades on, head down.

and we ride around town
listening to your favorite songs.

and we ride around town
while i think about what i
am doing wrong.

and we both know, i am
doing something wrong.

HONEST BY OMISSION

i keep a tin of breath mints in
my **car**, and spray

you told me
since you stopped smoking
the smell of it on others
is stronger

you smell it on me
though i said i quit

and **dammit**
i hate arguing
it is so annoying.

this is easier
keeping this stuff here

so, that is why
the car smells
intense
the heat exploded my
last spray bottle to bits

but if i roll the windows down
it really
ain' t that bad.

EVEN IF I LEFT, WHERE WOULD I GO?

this coffee is burnt
but still warm

so, it's still a lifesaver
in my eyes.

my throat is burnt
again, **dammit**—those cigarettes.

petti coats
sausage rolls
and train beers

i am not sure
how i got here

on a black leather couch
cursing a
peach schnapps hangover

while my 'lover' is
in the kitchen
making toast.

i feel gross.
in the same clothes from
nearly two days ago

i sit up
look around and
decide it would be best

if i just go.

i throw on my coat
and look around for
my purse, as you

emerge from
the **kitchen**
holding two plates.

i sit
down
and eat
my lunch.

BUT I ALREADY TOOK MY BRA OFF

stopping over for
just (one)

leant up against
my **kitchen** counters

you wipe beer from your chin
and ask, all proudly
"because of me?"

i try to read your face
figure out
what you are on about

but i can' t, so i become defensive
acting offended, i snarl
"what is?"

raising your eyebrows, you smirk

then blow air through your nostrils and
pick up your beer, pointing at
the magnets on my fridge, and say
"united"

i snatch the magnet down
hiding it between my hands

87

then glare at you
"i' ve always liked them. "

again, with your
fucking smirk.

you take a
long look at me
then slur out
"sure sure, love. "

i put the magnet in my **pocket**
take a gulp of my beer
and blurt out
"you are
full of yourself, darling. "

you put down your beer
cross the kitchen
and demand
i loosen up.

THAT GOOD WEED

*"painkillers
make me itchy"*

i say, as you shoved
the bag of pills
back into your **pocket**

handing me
the blunt

and gripping
my knee.

i had a bruise
forming on my ass
from losing russian roulette
(couch edition)

this one is
made of bricks
and i just sat on it like
the sloppy lush i am.

*"at least you don' t have to worry
about becoming a pill head"*
you said, as i laid
my head back, gently.

i took a deep **breath**
and held it in
for a minute
before letting the smoke
escape
then explained
"i was pretty hardcore
into adderall
back in the day."

you didn't say anything.

"i know, i am
super cool," i add.

you laughed, and i carried on
"got good grades
and skinny, fun times."

you told me to
"shut the fuck up"
and took back your blunt.

i laughed
then smiled

i could no longer
feel my ass.

THE HOMECOMING

flame to ash
lips to paper

a drag and deep
breath later, i
pull back and
listen for the
draft between the two

to rise with
thc and melodies

the ones that
hold me tight

and tell me
things are
somewhat
all right.

YOU ARE

red cheek tempered
and smug
i took a nug from the
plastic baggy laying on your
lap
broke it in half
putting some in the bowl
lit it, hit it
then sat back with
your bong in my hand

you held out yours
i gave it over
closed my eyes
started to **listen.**

i like it
so much

you are busy with
the trees

air goes **silent**

and i can finally think.

WHEN YOUR BIRTHDAY IS 11 DAYS AFTER CHRISTMAS

for my 8th
the nutcracker was in
town and my ma
wanted me
to see it

told me to pick
2 friends
and put
on my best skirt.

standing on
the grassy lawn
in front of the
auditorium, she took
our picture

then ushered us in
and when the intermission came
and she handed us all sodas.

talking about the show
i asked
"why don' t they talk. "

she went **silent**

93

tilted her head, and said
*"they just don' t, it' s
a ballet."*

i pressed my
lips together
like i still do today

and
sighed
like i still do today

*"oh, well, how much
longer is it,"* i asked.

looking at her watch
then towards the parking lot
*"that was it
it' s over."*

i smiled

asked if we could
go to
the beach
on the way
home.

THIS GUY I LIKE

flicking through
pictures of
my high school days

you say
"who's ryan? he looks gay."

turning the book around
so i could see

it was me and him
standing next to
scooby-doo at
universal studios

i smiled.
you threw the book down
snarling
"you like that kind of guy?"

pushing me
into
the **couch** cushions

i laughed, as you
grabbed
the

hair off
my neck and
bit down on
my earlobe.

"no!" i screeched.

you let
all your weight
come down on me

though
all i could really feel
was your penis

bruising
my thigh.

MAYBE I SHOULD GET SOME WEIGHTS

pop the top for me
i need a drink and
i' m too weak
but you are strong
you always are:

open a jelly jar
lift the heavy end of our **couch**
pick me up when i have too much
throw me down when i want it
throw me down when you want it
hold back branches when
we **sneak** around
knead nots from my shoulders
pound questions into me
force my temples to throb
rob the pride from my arms
push me away
then pull back, if i
try to escape.

THE FARM AT NIGHT

naked
awake
next to you, you sleep
you can always sleep

but i, i need more weed
and like a creep
no peeps
i **sneak**

in a shirt we got free
from a pub crawl, no panties

to the drawer
below our tv

pull out papers
and search for a bud

bumping into dried up batteries
and pipes

and old xbox games
though you gave the console away

i sway into the bathroom wall as
i close the door, quietly, **i think**

on the counter
i smoke until i feel tired

the doob ends
i still feel wired.

back in bed, i give up
start running monologues through
my head (i am a dog)
my mistakes are sheep

and when the light
starts to peek, i too
am finally
asleep.

I AM DROWNING OR I MISS MY DAD

put your hand up my skirt

i like that, apparently.

on my bed
sitting with legs open
i am broken and
you know it.

we talk about my dad.
we talk about why **i think**
maybe i'll be sad for
the rest of my life, i am
convinced of that.

it's ok, **it's ok**··· you say that

over
and
over
and

i just don't believe you.

tell me, i am screwed.
tell me, i never would have
been here without him.

BATTLE LOST

it was a tedious task—
to kill a fern

especially one that
lived quite happily on
an abandoned table.

the whole porch
had been forgotten
neighbors say, i smoke
too much

their 17 and 19-year-olds are
impressionable

but
it' s ok

i just started to keep my
doors closed

only opening them for
the **cats** to go
in and out.

my apartment filled
like lungs

some smoke escaped
most didn' t
and i baked

my clothes
my hair
the couch
the picture frames
the carpet, all smells of
green.

and when they finally moved
i reinstated territory

on the bottom floor
of a two-story

no yard but least
i got my porch back

the fern died in
the process, guess i

won
the war.

YOUR POEM DOESN'T RHYME

it takes two hits
in the spot above
the return button

i use my fist
the typewriter lets out a hiss.

i get it
you're old
you're tired of
ones like me
disregarding protocol
and property

headphones in
lights on everywhere
front door unlocked
tv blares
from the background for the **cats**
i regularly drop ash
then blow it away into the keys.

and since i can no longer see
the ash, it doesn't exist.

sometimes, i get asked
how i **sleep** at night…

...so, i tell them that.

ACCORDING TO WEBSTER

i used to wait
and then
things never came

so now i
don' t.

that is how
simplicity
works.

it' s not about
giving into
whatever obligation might
have you self-dissolved

it' s about
doing what
drifts you

to
sleep
at
night.

MY NEIGHBOR IN 312

i wonder what the
elephant looks like

the one that lives above me
and only moves at **night**

chasing marbles
and moving furniture
while doing so.

i am sure
it must be hard
to move around in such
a place, for an elephant

i can only think that
he must love the **sea**
and is happy anywhere near

even in the 2/2
apartment
above me
chasing marbles at 3am.

oh, i do hope
he is happy (since)
i am not.

AFTER IT ALL

driftwood lost at **sea.**

to whoever finds me there
carve **me** into art.

TO EARTH

sometimes

there is
too much
gravity
for
me to
feel high

and i

i get so
bummed out
when you
treat me
like the **moon**, knowing
damn well
i like
space
and would rather
be surrounded by

smoke rings.

it is noon
and you have
called four times, knowing

damn well
it snowed
last night
in florida.

i have
only just
laid my
head down.

in circles

i go in
circles
with you—

i just wanna float.

THAT HOUSE BEHIND TACO CITY

listen, i say

i gotta pee
but the bathroom
is occupied

i'm gonna go
to the beach.

i fucking hate jell-o shots
and i fucking hate you
for telling me to have some.

finger them first
then suck it all down
you said.

(what a joke)

i stumble off
thinking
this breeze feels nice
my cheeks are hot
you are hot

thinking
the **moon** looks cool

wish i could
get a decent photo.

i zip up my pants
make my way back
inside to find you

tell you, i love parties

they are so loud
i can' t hear
my finicky thoughts.

i want to **dance.**

but first
let' s have another shot

the blue
really wasn' t too bad.

PUTTING UP

if it weren' t for
cannabis, i think i
would have gotten
bored of this by now

how
ever
what
ever

i am not
and i
continue
to **dance.**

i
am
a
robot

here with bent arms
performing for

the people i
don' t even want
reading between
these lines.

if it weren' t for
cannabis, i might
have enough
brain cells left

to
just

shut up.

WEDDINGS, FUNERALS, & LIFE

"you' ll always need a
nice outfit, so **shut up**

and buy the damn **shoes** *for*
thirty dollars. "

THE NEWS SAYS IT'S PAST YOUR BEDTIME

losing
entire generations
to petty hesitations

is all i have
ever known, but

i still wanted
to try and relate
i still wanted
to try and think of

all the things i have
and you ··· don't.

i still wanted
to try and wear
your **shoes**, see what
it is like to
not know
what that means.

i still wanted
to try and make
myself **understand**
what lucky, really is.

115

i am 29
you are 7

i have always had a home
and yours dissolved
before you could talk.

i still wanted
to try and relate
but i am fearing, i think i

might be too late.

hopefully tomorrow will
be different, but

that' s just me
being ignorant
being hopeful

tomorrow is
never different.

maybe
i should
pray?

IT'S ALL IN MY HEAD ANYWAYS

i **understand** that your words
are not for me

even when they contain
syllables that sound
a **hell** of a lot
like my name

it's all for you
i get that, and

i get what i say
to you in an
angry state

it's too late
those are my words

they are about me
i am angry
with myself

but when you say
nice things

i will
pretend

they are for me

i will pretend
i said them myself

and it's ok for
you to not get that

—i am already
pretending you do.

hello my friends
i see you are back
again
in my head
in my bed
hell, i catch you guys
on the highway
while i smoke
you toke, and poke me
like maybe, i' ll catch on **fire.**
oh, good sires
you are hired!
don' t fret
don' t feel threat
i need you all
just as much as

you need me.

BRAT BEHAVIOR

ok. yes, i am high
but i swear, it looks
like it might be
on **fire**—please!

let me go check
one more time.

sighing, fighting the urge to just
get up and leave me, you
said, *"fine. "* i was
already across the room

inspecting the incense
making sure the distance
from it to the books was
agreeable enough for me

and it was, i sat back down
reached for the doobie in
the **ashtray**, but you told me to stop

i' ve had a lot
maybe too much, you insisted.

i grabbed it anyways.

PUFF PUFF POEM

my ma would have never
done this, since i was
her only ally, but i
heard all the stories.
many cautionary tales
from my gals
from my ma's pals
and sometimes from my ma's
very own mouth

the whole, pipe down
or i'll pull over and
let ya walk home, alone

maybe it was dark
and a bad neighborhood, how tragic.

leaving snotty little brats on
the roadside if they decide
acting up is an option

actually
i think you should do it.

oh, i am always so fickle
i never know where i will

...end.

listen
to the
rain trickle.

left my
doobie burning in
the **ashtray** and
went to
the fridge, i hope
i have pickles.

little
by
little

things
stopped being
so
serious.

WORD PLAY

caught my attention when
you nibbled on my ears
with your drawn-out vowels.

i dropped my jaw, but kept
quiet in fear, if i made a peep
you might have **stopped.**

that dictionary **tongue**
laid out a minefield
of goosebumps

my eyes fled
towards my brain for
safe keeping.

I DON'T KNOW WHAT TO SAY

an assembly of
words crowd my **tongue**, but none dare
                to jump from the **edge**.

BEGGARS CAN'T BE CHOOSERS

i saw blood first
i saw blood, then decided
it was real
i saw blood, then decided
it was real—my dad is dead.

scraping my way through
disposable fabric to
scream out, *"nurse!"*

"we need a nurse, please!"

i clench to the shirt of
a man i don't know
i clench to the shirt of
my brother

(we are lost)

i clench to the uniform of
a company that won't care
when it's morning, we mourn
and they move on.

holding on, pretending it's
the thing keeping me

from the edge, the thing that keeps
everyone from the **edge**

head into cotton balls, i **beg**

i beg, for a life that
isn' t even mine, for one that
came well before
any of my opinions.

i begged
there between
the breaths of others

i begged
there between
the thoughts and
robots of all this

i begged
to a god
i regularly mocked and
docked pay from

and then sat there
with audacity, thinking

i am being looked over.

NO SHOW

waiting
on sidelines
with sticky, tangerine hands
and open
potato chip bags
between the knees

waiting
watching for me
to breakdown

*"it has to
come soon"*
&
*"i can see it
in her eyes"*

spread through the
crowd, they **beg** for it
they want it

it'll be good
for me, i am told.

but i already
had it, privately

during the
shampoo and cream rinse of
my **day**, which is ok.

it is ok
to not be ok

at least
that is
what i am told.

DAMN CATS RUIN EVERYTHING

every **day**
at dawn

i pop
the **coffee** on

then the tv
used to be the news

but now it' s documentaries
something about animals in
africa, usually

then roll a doobie.

and for 30 minutes
that' s what i do.

then i shower, dress
get my things and
climb in the car.

i don' t have far to go
but it' s work

and on the way there
i always see the same cat

sitting under
a truck

smacking
its jaws

licking
its balls.

i stare
he stares back

and lately
i'm feeling like

maybe
it's me

i am the one
wasting all my time.

BREAK DANCE

the **coffee** has gone cold
and black
with a bitter taste

one from a lack of
sugar and substance.

slowly detaching
i let ash float in the cup
adding character.

*"you like things with
    character!"*

voices shout that
from my head

they try to convince me:
breathe
talk
walk
think nice things

but it' s too hard

i was hoping **autopilot**
would have kicked in by now.

131

GRIZZLY BEAR

i' m
like that:

on
auto
pilot

obligated
and mandated
to routine
it seems

like everyone else
gets to stay **awake**

and i
fight sleep.

THE HAPPIEST MAN I KNOW

monday through friday
it was
awake at 5

then drive to **work**
come home at 9.

on the weekends
it was
awake at 6

then eat a bowl of peas
read the paper
mow the lawn.

white socks up to
his knee

bite your tongue
if you called them
knee-highs

a
winston
red
hanging from
his lip

133

he was a
hardworking man.

and if
you ever
forgot

i am sure

he would have
fix that, too.

THE RULE OF THIRDS

rest a third
work a third
live a third

it would
sound reasonable if
that third bit
wasn' t being

taken for
every cent
of lunch money
hidden away
in its little
zipped up
cargo shorts.

taken for
a lesser third
than the others.

taken for
a fool.

i explained this
to you
between

sips of tequila
and coke

such a
horrible taste.

i said
this is what
brought me
over
to yours

we needed to
live more
and everything else
a little less.

possibly we don' t go
separate ways
possibly we don' t do
what others say.

and then you pointed out
that i probably shouldn' t
drive drunk
again.

YOU WANNA KNOW WHAT I THINK?

starting to prepare for
a night out:
staring at myself in a
mirror covered in
toothpaste splatter
and greasy fingerprints
i think of how my face has changed
and i feel like it's
grown into itself
and i feel like i'm looking better
with age
and i feel quite pleased
with this
i think of how one of
my friends were just
showing an article
around work about
the benefits of loving yourself
i didn't read it, simply because
i knew what it would say
the very thing i am
supposed to be practicing
technically i
should be toltec by now
pouring out with wisdom
but like most things i read
there is no devouring

137

it's always a skip
it's always a skim
it's always a well

here i go thinking of him···

i think of you
and as i take clumps of my hair
and **separate** them
taking each piece and
straightening them back in line

forgetting about any curls
i think of you

and how much you say you
love the process of things

and i wonder if
you were here
would you be enthralled
by this all?

closely watching my every move

as i break myself into parts
as i **build** myself into something

or would you be like you
always are—distant.

138

THE HELPER

```
brick.   mortar.   brick.   mortar.   brick
mortar.   brick.   mortar.   brick.   mortar.
brick.   mortar.   brick.   mortar.   brick.
mortar.   brick.   mortar.   brick.   mortar.
brick.   mortar.   brick.   mortar.   brick.
mortar.   brick.   mortar.   brick.   mortar.
brick.   mortar.   brick.   mortar.   brick.
mortar.   brick.   mortar.   brick.   mortar.
brick.   mortar.   brick.   mortar.   brick
mortar.   brick.   mortar.   brick.   mortar.
brick.   mortar.   brick.   mortar.   brick.
mortar.   brick.   mortar.   brick.   mortar.
brick.   mortar.   brick.   mortar.   brick.
mortar.   brick.   mortar.   brick.   mortar.
```

bit by bit
i watched you
build a **wall.**

bit by bit
i stood there
and helped.

MISERY LOVES COMPANY

i sit and tap

a little black fly
zips and zaps its
way around my room

i pause, stuck in myself
listening for the voices
to urge me on

but they' ve gone

and i start to wander
looking at pictures
and pieces of paper
i' ve pinned to the
wall, i see the fly again

next to a photo i took
in fall 2005, i stare

as it floats through the **air**
landing on my desk

whack!
now we' re the same.

AT IT

i get carried away

i do, usually with
your sentences

you say one thing
and i'll hear what i want;

ash in the **air**
you are over there
i am over here

silence and
your car **keys**
sit between us

and we both stare.

LOSING MYSELF

watching the typewriters on
my bookcase, waiting for
one to move
even slightly

and i would pounce.
it has been weeks since i could
be in this room for more than
5 minutes

and as i sit here
finally tasting the meat of
these **keys**
all i can think, just days ago,
i was completely
entranced by the idea of
smashing them all
with a baseball bat.
starving myself.

tiny debris of
screws and plastic, flying
everywhere.

maybe one would graze my eye
and i would end up in
the hospital

too—i' m so stupid;

i hope they blow up
and take my head off with
them

oh, i thought i was
over this;

i push down on keys like maybe
one will take me with it

i hope it' s Q

i would hate to feel
this guilt again
not spending enough time with Q

because out of
all the steps

i think **guilt**
feels the worse.

ONLY BORING PEOPLE GET BORED

twisting my hair
around my finger
it has gotten
so long

i keep going
until my wrist is
in there too, and
my hand is
knotted to
my scalp
i tug, it hurts—but i
like that;

across the room
my phone pings
i get up, go over

it is you
responding to
my text

3 days after the fact
in fact, i have forgotten
about it, about you—until now

"you are STILL smoking?"

i write back, i've quit.
(it is a lie)

you say, *"nice one."*

feeling the **guilt**, i admit i
still smoke when i am wasted, but
they taste like shit

don't know why
i do it

guess i just like things in my mouth
i send you a wink.

"jesus christ, christie"

"what?" i text back, feigning
        innocence.

*"you can't say things like that
to me,"* you admit.

interested, i pour myself some **wine**
and respond,
*"you aren't a child
you can handle it."*

might roll a doob
get some snacks, too.

145

one second i am
moving about like
nothing is wrong

dipping a soapy
sponge into a
wine glass

then i go still

stuck in
the glue of you

disappointed in
things that aren't
even close to what
a point looks like.

i am sliding back
but it also could be
forward.

what's this address?

DEATH & TAXES

inevitabilities
are the things
you should be
watching out for

crawling
laughing
deceiving

blink your
eyes as much
as you would like

they don' t
come fast

it' s a
slow process

happening while you
fuss over evening tv shows

and which man you would
rather give a blow.

happening while you
try out spontaneity

147

loosening the roots that
once kept you stable.

happening while you
wiggle

feeling free
feeling safe
and warm.

happening while you
are already **stuck.**

happening while you
start to struggle.

happening while you
beg, "**no!**"

BOO HOO HOO

sneaky
sneaky

you sneak
and i don' t even
have to wait

or peek
or think
of ways to catch you.

no
no
you know, i already know
where the up goes
and
down
down
down we go.

there is
only room enough
for one rat
in these walls

it' s me, me, **always** me.

THE NUMBERS GAME

3
oh
screw off 3

you are **always**
coming at me

tryin' me.

there seems to be

either me
alone

or
all of us
three

and you see
i don' t like that

i want it to be
just us **two.**

2
it' s me and you
and whenever

there is
one more

it makes me
feel blue

and though
you act like
it' s not true

we
both know

you
like it
better
too

when it' s
just us

2.

LET'S HAVE TEA

chit
chat
pitter
patter

the sound of
two hearts that
think they don't
matter

mad
hatter

let's have a
look at what
consumed you
whole

and then
i will **show**
you inside
what
got me.

LEARNING FROM A MISTAKE

when you say
let' s keep
this even

... i think of steven.

and how
he had always
been
kind of an
ass

i don' t like that.

i especially
don' t like being
on the
bottom when
it all
becomes uneven

i' d rather you
show me
what you got

then **sit back** and
you watch me try

not as hard
but you will
enjoy it.

i don' t like even
i never liked steven

but i like
you

and i want
you

to want
me

more
than
i want you.

"allie never cared about you"

i say that, then **sit back**
removing a throw pillow
it was hers, i'm sure.

you say something about
the shitty wiring in
your apartment, how you bought
at least a hundred lightbulbs
in the past few years.

i look around, purple drapes
salt and pepper microfiber
sectional couch
a picture of you two in cancun
and one of buddah

"you should
sell your stuff
get new stuff
get a new place. "

you ask why that
matters, that you were
talking about
the **lights**, that i am

off topic.

"i know"

i said, then went on to
tell you how
allie doesn' t think about
you, anymore.
and i am concerned, since

i think you
think about

only her.

you called me a bitch

then laughed
sorta
kinda

it could have been a growl, anyhow

what are
friends for?

MAKE BELIEVE YOU ARE YOUR OWN PERSON

we are 8

and outside
playing, suns up
streetlights off.

i say, let's be animals

i am a cat
meow!

what are you?

you say, cat

meow?

and i say, "*fine*"
though, ya know, you can be
any animal you want

don't **settle** for my dream
don't settle for anything.

ANXIETY GETS ME DRUNK

stones skip across the
glassy fields of my eyes
and you sigh

the hazy atmosphere in here
has become obsolete
my body glazed over.

you ask if
i am fucked up enough.

i **settle** further into
the couch
and **reply** that i
have never felt more clear

i finally feel
sober.

LESS WHINE MORE WINE

in your car:

i lit a cigarette
while you fidgeted with
your phone

flipping past songs
 *"i don' t get pandora
if i play the
blind pilot station*

*i want to
hear blind pilot. "*

i **reply**
 *"if you wanted the album
you should just
download spotify. "*

giving me an unimpressed eye
you said, through gritted teeth
 "i like pandora. "

i didn' t
suggest
anything else.

staring out
the window

watching
the birds

how they fly

wondering why

one of the flock is
hanging back

alone

i decided
right then

it is
my favorite one.

THE BREAKUP NOTE I LEFT FOR MY EGO

you said
i was too obtuse

that i
wasn' t getting you

that i
didn' t agree with your
point of view

that i
refuse to get a clue

that i
am too including of
everyone else
but you.

i' m too inclusive, what
do you mean?

haven' t you seen
what happens to
the people left **alone**

they turn blue.

so, you
with an
exclusive
reclusive
kind of view

i won' t
be intrusive
i won' t
conclude either

i just wish
you well

and want you
to know

my open **door**
is here, hoping

you
make it
back through.

WHITE GIRL WASTED

i didn' t before
but i do now:

i close the **door** behind
me when i enter the spare
bedroom to type about
the things i like to
think about

the things i don' t think
you think about

and when it starts to
hurt too much i
give myself a
subtle **push** to
hurry
and get
the good things out

the things i think you
need to hear the most.

BEACH BABY

kiss me like the sea:
slap my lips with hunger and
push my **lungs** to breathe.

THE FEAR OF WANTING SOMETHING

you have
done a lot of
strange things

admit it.
and i

i admit it

sitting
on a
barstool
thinking

you play
your sax so well

you have
such big **lungs**

i think
i think i like you

yet, once
i pretended
i didn' t
know you

you had your cat
i had my cat
and we both sat

silent in a
vet office—
waiting room

pretending

i
don' t
know
you

lie!
and now
i am thinking

why do i
do such weird things?
why am i
wanting you?
why do i
feel a tad bit blue?

i shouldn' t
even like you.
but, fuck - i do.

BETRAYAL: THE GOLDEN SHOWER

port-o-potty wafts
behind me, i forgot to
prepare myself

a 12-ounce plastic cup
fell from the
slanted shelf

hit the ground
splashed into my face

i felt that
i was worth it

i took it
thinking

everyone else
has experienced worse.

i'm the worst, the one
pretending

no one has
had it
worse than me.

YOU ARE DRUNK

i forgot
my keys
and left you
at the bar:

so, when i
got home

i had to
pee outside of
our spare bedroom
window

so, i am
thankful of
the stairs
they protected me
and i know

i fucking
know!

i complain about them, i say
they are
the **worse,** those ones
above us

so, tonight
they saved **me**
they shielded me
they serenaded my privacy
keeping embarrassment
from the street

so, shut the
front door
close the
sliding glass one, too

we are
going to bed

i
just don' t care
how loud
our neighbors are.

MUNCHIES FOR THE ZOMBIES

i have
a lot
of questions

and i am not sure
who i start with

my childhood
or the people
who lied to me.

why
oh, why
is everyone i know dying?

tell **me**

is it because
i know more people now
or is it because
the quality of company i keep
diminished

tell me

why
is everyone i know dying

tell me

when i was 5
no one died
now at 30
there is a new one
every morning, mourning
overdoses
old age
on the way home
had an accident

or the hospital
i know a few
sent away
to lay alone
and the doctors say
"oh, how could we have known?"

tell me

is it me
or is everyone **you know**
dying too?

AIRHEAD ANXIETY

i am in bed
under the covers

and i have been there a while
so, **you know** it' s warm

and my pillow hasn' t
been flipped yet
i am trying to trap
all that i got (in)

fluffy socks
sweatpants
a hoodie

the a/c has been off for days
and the windows closed up

still
i am shaking
i am shivering
i am praying
to anything that might listen

i am closing my eyes, thinking
of something on fire

still
nothing works

and i know
nothing will work;
nothing ever works

until it' s
already working

which is
perfect, because

all i know how
to do

is
lay
and wait.

THERE IS NO END

you started it.

sat on your bed in
the back room of a
six-lad flat, you were
teaching me how to
roll spliffs and i
hadn' t quite gripped that
the sticky bit was
the key

got to get it **perfect**
got to get it down and as much as
possible, fast.

my **favorite** part has
always been the rip
the separation, the glue
the··· *"will this stick or
         am i screwed, again. "*

it took me a few times
it took me a few packs
of skins and
some patience on
your part but
eventually

174

we moved outside into
the dark and you passed over
a lighter, saying
 "rollers rights. "

that seemed fair

i lit it
i hit it

then coughed up
bits of
my heart.

MUTUALLY MEH

you get drunk
and play
these masterpieces

from bach
and beethoven

and even that one
song by
debussy
because you know
it's my **favorite**

been in a few movies
i relate with

and at the end of it all
that is what you are
trying for

trying to
relate to me

and anyone in this room
that will listen

but they won't

they are
huddled around
the porch

smoking a **joint**.

and you
you want to
relate to yourself

but
you don' t know
who that is anymore.

and neither do i.

and neither does my mother.

or anyone
anymore.

but that doesn' t
matter to me

just please
don' t stop
playing.

THE CALIFORNIAN MOUNTAINS

you are always asking me
to take my pants off
30 degrees and we are
outside trying to light a
doob, you grab my ass
and ask me to pull my
jacket up, you are
feeling wild and
want a feel
i roll my eyes and move away
swaying into a wooden fence
you laugh
and i finally get the **joint** lit
you dick
but i **admit**, i like it

and back inside
freezing
tensed up
i ask for a back rub

you tell me to
take my pants off
and we all know, a deal
is a deal—
i take it all off
lay down, relaxed

probably from
the weed.

PARTICIPATION

it is all gospel
with a steeple
and a church
and people

there are so many people
i wonder when
they will all go away

i am only
trying to say

i like being alone
and i like
being with everyone else, too

just lately
there is no alone

snowbirds fly in
and my head starts to spin

and my bike wheels
spin more, too
because i can' t
drive anywhere, anymore;

i think you should
really retest drivers
over the age
of 70, they aren't
trustworthy

it is
super scary.

i **admit**
this is what
i would say if
my sermon
got a chance

if i am here
i might as well
play.

DEFLATE GATE

my hands smell like
your penis
and the thing is
i like it.

looking at myself in
your mom's bathroom mirror
i notice an eyelash
on my cheek
go to pick it off
then pause

wash
my hands
first

now they smell like
vanilla.

i know you don't get pink eye
that way

but sometimes
it's best to
play it **safe.**

THAT DRUNK GIRL

i get why
they are worried

i am stumbling
over nothing and

just dropped my phone onto
a wood table

it made a
bang
a flop, a

i don' t know
where i am.

some guy says hey
it' s not **safe**

you' ve had enough
stop trying to leave

i laugh
thinking

i love how weird i am
making this.

hey
how big is
your peen?
come closer

my blood is curling
my head has curdled

i am bad
i am so sad

i would be glad
if you came

on me
over me
around me

please just
make it
me

me
me
me.